A Robbie Reader

Donovan McNabb

THE STORY OF A FOOTBALL STAR

by
Joanne Mattern

Mitchell Lane
PUBLISHERS

P.O. Box 196
Hockessin, Delaware 19707
Visit us on the web: www.mitchelllane.com
Comments? email us: mitchelllane@mitchelllane.com

Printing   3   4   5   6   7   8   9

A Robbie Reader

Library of Congress Cataloging-in-Publication Data
Mattern, Joanne, 1963-
    Donovan McNabb / by Joanne Mattern.
        p. cm. — (A Robbie reader)
    Includes index.
    ISBN 1-58415-294-X (library bound)
    1. McNabb, Donovan—Juvenile literature. 2. Football players—United States—
    Biography—Juvenile literature. 3. McNabb, Donovan. 4. Football players. 5. African
    Americans—Biography.   I. Title. II. Series.
    GV939.M38M38 2005
    796.332'092--dc22
                                                                                2004009300

ABOUT THE AUTHOR: Joanne Mattern is the author of more than 100 nonfiction books for children. Along with biographies, she has written extensively about animals, nature, history, sports, and foreign countries. She lives near New York City with her husband and two young daughters.

PHOTO CREDITS: Cover: Streeter Lecka/Getty Images; p. 4 Ezra Shaw/Getty Images; p. 6 Mark Lennihan/AP Photo; p. 8 Rick Stewart/Getty Images; p. 9 http://www.philly.com; p. 10 top: Miles Kennedy/AP Photo; bottom: Alex Brandon/AP Photos; p. 12 Ted S. Warren/AP Photos; p. 14 Winslow Townson/Getty Images; p. 16 Doug Pensinger/Getty Images; p. 18 Ezra Shaw/Getty Images; p. 20 top: Doug Peninger/Getty Images; bottom: Jamie Squire/Getty Images; p. 22 Ezra Shaw/Getty Images; p. 23 Jamie Squire/Getty Images; p. 24 Thos Robinson/Getty Images; p. 25 Ronald Martinez/Getty Images; p. 26 Brad C. Bower/AP Photo; p. 28 Douglas M. Bovitt/AP Photo; p. 29 http://www.donovanmcnabb.com.

TABLE OF CONTENTS

Donovan cheers after he throws a touchdown to win the football game when the Philadelphia Eagles played the New York Giants in November, 2003.

AN UNPOPULAR CHOICE

Donovan McNabb sat in Madison Square Garden in New York City. Thousands of people were there for the National Football League's 1999 draft. Every year, NFL teams pick new players in the draft.

Many people wanted the Philadelphia Eagles to pick a player named Ricky Williams. Williams had won an award called the Heisman (HYZ-man) Trophy. Every year, the Heisman Trophy is given to the best college player.

The Eagles did not choose Williams. Instead, they picked Donovan McNabb. When the crowd heard Donovan's name, a huge roar filled Madison Square Garden. The crowd was not cheering. Instead, people were booing.

Donovan shows off his new Eagles football jersey after being chosen to play on the team. Eagles fans were not excited, but Donovan and his family and friends were very happy.

Donovan was surprised that people were so unhappy. He felt angry, but he did not let his feelings upset him. Donovan walked up on the stage with a big smile on his face. He was happy and proud that the Eagles had chosen him for their team. Most of all, he knew he could show everyone that the Eagles had made the right choice.

Donovan gets ready to make one of his great passes to a teammember.

Donovan enjoys playing football as well as watching his teammates play.

NOT WELCOME HERE

Donovan Jamal McNabb was born on November 25, 1976. He was born in Chicago, Illinois. His parents are Samuel and Wilma McNabb. Sam worked for a power company in Chicago. Wilma was a nurse. Donovan also has a brother named Sean (SHAWN). Sean is four years older than Donovan.

Donovan's parents, Samuel and Wilma, are very happy to see their son succeed as a football player.

9

Donovan enjoys sharing laughs with his friends from other teams after a game.

When Donovan and Sean were young, the family moved to Dolton, Illinois. The McNabbs were one of the first African-American families in Dolton. They did not receive a warm welcome. Strangers smashed the windows of their house. They painted insulting words on the house. They broke into the house and kicked holes in the walls. By doing these hateful things, people thought they could scare the McNabbs out of town.

The McNabbs refused to be chased from their home. Sam McNabb taught his sons that if they were nice to other people, then others would be nice to them. Donovan took his father's advice. He made friends with the other children in the neighborhood. He was fun to be around and had a great sense of humor. Soon people stopped bothering the McNabbs.

This is Frank Lenti, the football coach at Mt. Carmel High School.
Donovan helped lead Mr. Lenti's team to the state championships.

"PLEASE, MOM!"

Donovan loved sports. The walls of his room were covered with pictures of sports stars. Football was his favorite sport.

Donovan decided he did not just want to watch football. He wanted to play it. He tried out for the football team at Mt. Carmel High School and made the team.

However, Donovan's mother did not want her son to play. She said Donovan was too skinny for such a rough sport. Donovan begged his mother to let him play. Finally, the team's coach called Wilma. He promised her that Donovan would not get hurt. After a long phone conversation, Wilma finally said yes.

CHAPTER THREE

Donovan throws a pass while playing for Syracuse University.

Donovan was an important part of Mt. Carmel's football team. He played on the school's basketball team, too. He was a good player in both sports. He was also a clown. The school coaches told Donovan's mother that he was always fooling around. Wilma agreed. She said Donovan told her, "If I can't have fun doing something, what's the point of doing it?"

Donovan was such a good athlete that he won a **scholarship** to Syracuse (SARA-cyoos) University in Syracuse, New York. Donovan played football and basketball at Syracuse. During his third year at college, he decided to play just football. This was a good decision!

Donovan was named Big East **Rookie** of the Year in 1995. He was the Syracuse team's captain in 1998. He was also chosen as the Big East **Conference offensive** player of the year three times. By the time he graduated in 1998, Donovan held many school and Big East records. Then it was time for the NFL.

Donovan runs the ball in for a touchdown.

PROVING HIMSELF

Donovan joined the Philadelphia Eagles in 1999. He knew he had to prove he deserved to be on the team. Donovan's father had always told him, "You have to be willing to work hard in life. Nothing comes easy."

Donovan exercised (EX-er-sized) and practiced. He worked with coaches and other players. Whenever he was on the field, he played as hard as he could.

Donovan did not play very much during his first season with the Eagles. He was the backup quarterback. This meant he only played when the starting quarterback could not. Even though he played only a few games, coaches

Donovan celebrates after he scores a touchdown for his team.

and other players liked what they saw. The team's head coach said Donovan was the fastest learner he had ever worked with.

In 2000, Donovan became the Eagles' starting quarterback. He started all the games that season. He had 3,365 passing yards, 330 complete passes, 21 touchdowns, and 13 interceptions.

Donovan showed he was a strong player. Still, some people did not think he deserved so much attention. In 2003, an announcer named Rush Limbaugh said that Donovan was not really a very good player. He said that the **media** (MEE-dee-uh) only said good things about Donovan because he was African-American.

Many people were very angry at Limbaugh's comments. Donovan did not say anything. He just kept on working hard and showing that he was a good player. "I play this game to be the best," he once said. "And the only sure way I know to be the best is to outwork everybody else . . . I'm never satisfied."

Donovan gets ready to pass the ball during one of the very first games that he played in the NFL.

Donovan leaps over other players to score a touchdown during his first season with the Eagles.

ON THE FIELD

Donovan played his first NFL game on November 14, 1999. The Eagles beat the Washington Redskins. Donovan was the first Eagles rookie quarterback to win his first NFL start in 28 years.

Donovan's first full season with the Eagles was in 2000. He played very well. He broke the team's record for the most touchdown tries and the most touchdowns. Donovan was named the NFL Player of the Year by CBS Radio. He also finished second in the voting for the Most Valuable Player of the season.

At the end of each football season, the best players are invited to play in the Pro Bowl. Donovan was chosen to go. He did not expect

A New York Giants player tackles Donovan as he tries to score a touchdown.

to play, because there were other quarterbacks who had more experience. Then quarterback Kurt Warner was injured. Donovan led his team to many touchdowns and had a great game!

2001 was another great season for Donovan. He threw 25 touchdown passes. That was more touchdown passes than he had ever thrown before. Donovan also became only the fourth quarterback in Eagles history to pass for 3,000 yards two seasons in a row. He played in the Pro Bowl again that year, too.

2002 started out well. Then disaster (diz-AS-ter) struck. The Eagles played the Arizona Cardinals in November. Donovan broke his ankle during the game. It was the first really bad injury he had ever had. He played half the game with a broken ankle. But then he could not play until his ankle got better. He only played 10 games that season.

When the 2003 season began, Donovan was ready to play. He had another great year. Donovan showed that he was a strong, smart player who could help his team succeed. But,

Donovan looks different in regular clothes than he does in his football uniform.

2004 turned out to be the best year of all for Donovan. He led the Eagles to win the NFC championship in January 2005. They beat Atlanta 27–10, which gave the Eagles their first Super Bowl appearance since January 1981! Donovan enjoyed his success. He was disappointed for the previous three seasons when the Eagles fell one game short each year of reaching the Super Bowl. But now they had made it. "This is a dream come true for me," Donovan said to the reporters.

After coming so far and trying so hard, however, the Eagles came up just short at the Super Bowl when they lost to the New England Patriots, 24–21. Donovan finished with three touchdown passes and three interceptions, but he was still sad they lost.

While his ankle was injured in 2002, Donovan couldn't play. Here he is sitting on the sidelines, cheering for his teammates.

Donovan talks to reporters about his new 12-year contract with the Eagles.

GIVING BACK

Donovan's football skills have made him very rich. In 2002, he signed a new contract with the Eagles. The contract was worth $50 million. In spite of his riches and fame, Donovan remains a hardworking, humorous person who wants to live a regular life.

Donovan does a lot more than just play football. In 2003, he married Raquel-Ann (RACK-ell) Nurse. Raquel is also called Roxi (ROCKS-ee). She was a basketball star at Syracuse University. She and Donovan had dated since college.

Donovan gives a lot of time and money to charity. His grandmother died from a disease called **diabetes**. Donovan's father and brother

Donovan enjoys giving his time to charities. While playing Santa Claus at the Ronald McDonald House in Philadelphia, he is able to make children very happy during the Christmas season.

also have diabetes. Donovan is the national (NASH-ih-null) spokesperson for the American Diabetes Association. In 2000, he made the Donovan McNabb Foundation. The money raised by the foundation helps people with diabetes and their families. Every year, Donovan holds a celebrity (se-LEH-brit-ee) all-star weekend to raise awareness (uh-WHERE-ness) and money to fight this disease.

Donovan enjoys helping children too. Every Christmas he plays Santa at a community center in Philadelphia. Donovan also pays for children to go to summer camp. His actions show that Donovan is a leader both on and off the field.

Sean, Wilma, Samuel and Donovan pose for a picture together. Donovan's foundation helps people with diabetes.

1976 Donovan McNabb is born on November 25 in Chicago, Illinois.

1984 The McNabbs move to Dolton, Illinois, a suburb of Chicago.

1994 Donovan enters Syracuse University.

1995 Donovan is named Big East Rookie of the Year.

1998 Donovan serves as team captain of Syracuse University's football team; he is selected as Big East Player of the Year. He graduates from college with a degree in speech communications.

1999 The Philadelphia Eagles pick Donovan in the NFL draft on April 17. He plays in his first NFL game on September 19.

2000 Donovan establishes the Donovan McNabb Foundation.

2001 Donovan leads the Eagles to the NFL playoffs. He is named the Philadelphia Eagles Offensive Most Valuable Player for the second year in a row.

2002 Donovan signs a 12-year, $50 million contract with the Eagles.

2003 Donovan marries his college sweetheart, Raquel-Ann Nurse; he is named "Caring Athlete of the Year" by *USA Weekend*.

2004 Donovan leads the Eagles to the NFC Championship.

For Kids

Bradley, Michael. *Donovan McNabb.* Benchmark All-Stars. Tarrytown, New York: Benchmark Books, 2004.

Bradley, John Ed. "Eagle Scout." *Sports Illustrated for Kids,* July 30, 2001, Vol. 95, issue 4, page 58.

Cosgrove, Ellen. "Gonna Fly Now." *Sports Illustrated for Kids,* September 2001, Vol. 13, issue 9, page 41.

Wahl, Grant. "Ahead of His Class." *Sports Illustrated.* February 18, 2002, Volume 96, Issue 7, page 62.

Internet

Donovan McNabb, Official Web Site
http://www.donovanmcnabb.com

NFL.com: Donovan McNabb
http://www.nfl.com/players/playerpage/133361

Philadelphia Eagles
http://www.philadelphiaeagles.com/team/
teamRosterDetails.jsp?id=195

GLOSSARY

conference (KON-frens)—a group of teams

diabetes (dy-uh-BEE-teez)—a disease in which the body does not produce enough insulin, leading to too much sugar in the blood

media (MEE-dee-uh)—television, radio, magazines, and newspapers

offensive (ah-FEN-sihv)—in sports, the team or players who are trying to score

playoffs (PLAY-offs)—a series of games that determine which teams will play for the championship

quarterback (KWAR-tuhr-bak)—a football player who leads the offense

rookie (RUH-kee)—an athlete in his or her first season with a team

scholarship (SKAH-luhr-ship)—money given to someone to pay for school

INDEX